Amelia Walker has published two previous poetry collections: **Fat Streets and Lots of Squares** and **Just Your Everyday Apocalypse**. She has also written three books of poems, worksheets, games and lesson plans for the primary school classroom. These are part of Macmillan's **All You Need To Teach** series. Amelia is currently working on a fictocritical thesis about poetry for her PhD studies at the University of South Australia. **Sound and Bundy** was written as the artefact component of her Honours thesis.

Dear Liz,
Warm greetings from
Australia!
~Amelia

Interactive Press
Emerging Authors Series

Sound and Bundy

Amelia Walker

Interactive Press
Brisbane

Interactive Press
an imprint of IP (Interactive Publications Pty Ltd)
Treetop Studio • 9 Kuhler Court
Carindale, Queensland, Australia 4152
sales@ipoz.biz
ipoz.biz/IP/IP.htm

First published by IP in 2012
© Amelia Walker, 2012

Printed in 12 pt Cochin on 14 pt Bell Gothic Std.

National Library of Australia
Cataloguing-in-Publication entry:

Author: Walker, Amelia.

Title: Sound and bundy / Amelia Walker.

ISBN: 9781921869365 (pbk.)

Subjects: Working class--Poetry.

Dewey Number: A821.4

For Elliott Mundy.
Thank you for being an amazing friend...
and for taking me to the Malley exhibition at Heide.

Acknowledgements

Front Cover Image: Richard Steenvoorde

Jacket Design: David Reiter

Author Photo: Greg McInnes

Extra massive thanks to my university supervisors, Paul Skrebels and Vicki Crowley, and also to Graham Catt, Heather Taylor-Johnson, Jack Robins, Clare Woods, Ioana Petruscu, Glen Murdoch, Cam Black, Gabby Everall, the MaxMo crew, Steve Smart, Meg Dunn, Kris Terbutt, Eddy Burger, Randall Stephens, Greg McInnes and family, Achinta Gupta, Ashoke Gupta and family, all the other amazing poets in Adelaide, Melbourne, Kolkata & other places I have visited, the SA Writers' Centre, Carclew, the Australian Poetry Centre, my parents and my whole family, and last but definitely not least, Richard Steenvoorde and family.

Foreword

Three years ago I set out, quite innocently, to research a biography of recently deceased Australian poet, Jason Silver. I never suspected my actions would uncover perhaps the biggest scandal in Australian literature since the Ern Malley affair of 1944. The tale has, of course, been told to death by the tabloids so I shall here relate only the briefest possible version.

Like Malley, Silver never existed in the flesh but was the creation of three other poets, Pete Lind, Shannon Woodford and Angie Rawkins. The trio met at the Red Lion Readings, a monthly poetry open mike that ran from 1998 to 2006 at the Red Lion Hotel in Elizabeth, one of Adelaide's outer suburbs. Lind established the readings as well as the Red Lion Press, which published chapbooks by group members, Silver included.

Silver supposedly suffered Bipolar Disorder and committed suicide in December 2005, aged 34. His collected works, released early 2006, received resounding praise until the deception – for I disagree with the term hoax – came to light. Afterwards, Silver's poetry was dismissed as meaningless ramblings with too many quotes from other writers and musicians. The Red Lions were denigrated for their lax ethics, their lack of formal education and the performance-based nature of their writings. The attacks only ceased in the wake of another, unrelated scandal – the debates surrounding Friendly Street's so-called "Porno Poet".

Three years on, the publication of this anthology may seem odd. Surely everybody has moved on? Yet this is precisely why it is time to re-examine Silver and the other Red Lions. Now the initial outrage no longer skews judgment it is possible to view these poems objectively and recognise their merits. Regretfully, this recognition may come too late for Lind, who ended his life in December 2007, aged 38.

Before his death, Lind, along with the other Red Lions, adamantly rejected the comparisons between Jason Silver and Ern Malley. In his journal he wrote, "Jason was never meant to be uncovered. We weren't out to make a fool of anybody, we just wanted to explore."

Whatever the poems were, whatever they were not, they are here. The decision now rests in the hands of readers.

– Harrison Lomax, June 2009

Contents

Poems by Angie Rawkins

Poems by "Jason Silver"

Sound and Bundy

Pete Lind

1969 – 2007

Lind initiated and ran the Red Lion Readings and chapbook press. His mother and father were English migrants who moved to Australia because of work opportunities in the newly opened Holden car manufacturing plant. Lind also worked in the plant for several years, but became unemployed in 2003. He lived in a defacto marriage with fellow Red Lion Shannon Woodford from 1999 to 2005, during which time the couple had two children. Lind committed suicide in December 2007 and is deeply missed.

Bloody Poets, 1994

I am not a poet.
I'm just a guy who writes poetry, got it?
I can't stand poets,
the way they stare
out of books, yellow and sour.
As people they might have been okay,
good for a drink and a laugh.
Poor sods, getting turned into poets.
And thank God I am not one!
If I were I'd have to wear black
and speak strange unto thee
and shove my head in ovens
because I would hate myself
for being a poet,
a lie.
Lucky, then, I'm just a guy,
a guy who works,
who comes home
and goes out,
good for a drink and a laugh,
a guy who eats and shits
and sometimes can't shit,
who watches too much TV and doesn't care,
a guy
just like any guy
who, it just happens, writes poetry.

Girl Friday, 1994

She keeps leaving me.
Or I send her away.
Whichever, I always know she'll be back.
Two castaways, we can't help but drift
together. On Friday nights,
beneath the dim globes of our favourite bar,
she's sitting, waiting
for me to find her.

A master of disguise,
sometimes blonde, sometimes dark,
skin pale or tanned.
One week she is tall, the next short,
but I always know her
by her eyes.

She wears little grey ribbons in her eyes.

Above the chatter of pokies in the next room,
she plays her latest lucky name.
Sometimes Sonia, others Michelle
or Rona or Lisa or Kristy.
And what the heck,
I become different people for her too.
Keeps things interesting
for both of us.

I buy her a tequila sunrise
or a bourbon and coke or a gin and tonic
or a beer. She gives me a smile
or a snarl or a kiss on the cheek
or the neck or the mouth.

We go back to my place. Always my place.
I've thought about asking her why,
but then maybe it's me who insists,
who doesn't want to know
the colours of her walls her sheets the books on her shelves.

Inside all this civilised clothing
we are both savages,
our bodies foreign languages
we learn through points and gestures,
stutters and gasps.
Lisping children, we invent new games,
new words for only us and only now.

Next week we will have forgotten
on purpose,
will learn to speak all over,
discover ourselves savages again – and again –

This is why she leaves me.
This is why I send her away.

Bruises, 2006

(for Brian Lind, 1973-1996)

You were always strangely proud
of your bruises. Wore them like medals
and never went without decoration
whether learning to walk
or learning to fly
off the shed roof
—you swore you'd do it
one day
and though I was older and should have known better,
a small part of me believed you
because right from the start
there was something in your eyes
that soared higher than the things we can hold.

Sixteen you started talking about the Air Force,
set Mum into such a state
—awake all night, grinding her jaw to chalk—
though you, of course, never noticed,
already soaring miles beyond us
in your mind.

It was because of her they wouldn't let you in,
not that she planned it,
that night when you were just seven months
and fast asleep through the blur of streets
and stoplights, white sheets and stern faces,
that night when I learned, at four years old
that valium can't kill you.

But heroin can.

They put you in a grey suit,
long sleeves to cover your arms.
I didn't need to see to know
they were covered in bruises,
dull black decorations
from a different type of war.

The last time I saw you, six months before,
you said you were gonna get clean
of everything, even the booze,
and though I was older and should have known better
a small part of me believed you
because even with busted teeth and yellow skin,
there was still something in your eyes.
Those fucking eyes.

They're closed now,
no doubt eaten
by something that'll never tell me
if you ever did it,
if you learned to fly.

That Sort, 1998

I'm the sort you see at bus shelters,
the guy with the tatts and the faded black jeans,
the sort who pays the driver all in five cent pieces,
who gives up his seat for the blind girl
then stares and wonders what it'd be like to fuck her.

I'm the sort who actually enjoys baked beans on toast,
I'm not the sort who owns shares
or knows what they mean by negative gearing.
I'm the sort who pays bills – just –
and knows what they mean by black kiss.

I'm the sort who goes to church
every Christmas, to the wrestling
every time it's on,
the sort who believes it's all real
even though I know it's not.

I'm the sort who'll drink VB if I have to
(and yes, I'm the sort that has to).
Fuck Crows. Fuck Power.
I'm the sort who goes for Centrals,
the sort who really does read the articles in Penthouse,
but would never claim that's why I buy it.

I'm the sort who grew up eating dinner at six,
meat and no veg, fish and chip Fridays,
the sort who broke three noses before the end of year six,
who thought that was the way to get along.
I cried myself to sleep every night 'til I was seven,
then not at all for twenty two years.

I'm the sort who listens to the words in songs,
who listens to Metallica,
who listens to the blues.

I'm the sort your mother said watch out for,
the sort who wants to spend hours
just tasting your neck, unbuttoning your blouse.
I'm the sort who leaves before sun up,
the sort who still believes in love.

I'm the sort of person who tells the truth.
I'm the sort of person who lies.
I'm the sort of person who writes poetry,
the sort who can bench ninety-eight-point-five kilos.

I'm the sort of person who gets up and says all this
out loud, in the middle of the God damn Red Lion.
I'm the sort who sees the looks in your eyes,
but keeps on standing here, standing tall,
looking the fuck straight back and saying Yeah,
that's right,
I'm that sort of person.

She's Not My Type... 1998

...but I like her.
Much more than she likes herself.

I like her black dress, black boots, black looks, black hair
growing out blonde. I even like her black eyeliner
smudged from cheek to brow as she sits, shoulders slumped,
sipping black coffee in my kitchen,
flicking chips of black polish on the floor.
I like finding them later, tiny fragments that tell me
it was more than a dream. And the eyeliner too
on my pillow, a blurred print of her
watching me
blackly
– sealed tighter than any kiss.

I want to fuck her with the lights on,
but she refuses,
says she's ashamed
of being so big.
I say men have the opposite problem.

But it's hard to ignore the sniggers
and stares from friends who've known me years,
who know my type.

My type are blonde,
tight tops, tighter jeans.
My type have pink nails and suntans.
They like Robbie Williams and Midouri.
My type read their star signs in Cleo
or New Woman if they're really empowered.

When I try to lend them Fear and Loathing,
my type tell me they've always loved Gonzo
– but not as much as Big Bird.

No.
She's not my type.

What an Heirloom, 1999

By the time they found it your lungs were all but gone.

How long had you been hiding the pain
from yourself? Pretending to laugh, to sing
when you could barely breathe?
You must have carried it for years,
that black secret, slowly eating you –

but then, you always were good at silence.

"If you can't say anything nice..." you'd chime,
tuneful as the ice cream van,
with a smile pink as the sugar bomb sherbet
that landed me in the dentist's chair time
and time again.

"This tooth has to go," is not nice,
but sometimes it needs to be said.
Just like the word "Cancer",
just like that other word
I can't say, because it's not mine.
It was yours, except you never said it
Now it's buried with you,
buried alive.

But you did leave me plenty of silence.

My Monsoon Missus 1999

She says she feels like crying
because she just does.
Sometimes she feels like listening to music,
eating chocolate or having a bath.
Why should crying be different?

Her tears come from her body.
She feeds them as they grow
inside her. She births
and loses them, wobbly shards of self.
But while they are ploughing her cheeks
or nestling into her cracked, salty lips,
they are hers. Nobody can take them
or stop them
– not even me –

especially not me.

She says crying is not stealing
or murder or rape. So why
do people say she's bad?
She says she's sick
of being told she's sick,
of doctors who clog up her tear ducts
with salts that blur and sting.
She says it's jealousy.

She says I don't understand
and I say, No Shit.
I don't understand her taste in music, either,
but I let her play it
and if crying 'til the whole joint floods is what she needs
then I'll drown with her and die happy.

Grey Clouds, 2001

You're getting smaller,
you who once loomed so far above me,
shoulders wide as the sky,
eyes grey as storm clouds,
the lightning fully loaded.

Now you need nurses
to unscrew the beers
I bring every month
when I visit you in your little room
with its stains, its stink

of piss and pine-o-clean.
Four walls, one window
looking onto a wall.
Your world is shrinking too.
I am a good son. I must be

because I visit and bring you beer.
On the drive home
I find myself laughing
– softly at first, then louder –
in the mirror I discover

my grey eyes grown larger
as this thing I never dreamed I'd feel
stirs thicker inside me
like her tumor,
like thunder, a storm.

Melbury Street, 2002

And so again, after one beer more than I should've
– though mind you, not half what I could've –
I find myself stumbling dark streets,
crossing to the other side
of the train line. I find myself standing here,
wide mouthed, on Melbury Street.

Melbury Street: nineteen years, three dogs
and one skateboard us kids all fought over
'til it broke. Melbury Street: my first bike,
first car, first kiss in the back seat, first slap
across the face, but soon after, yes, that first.
Melbury Street: living two doors down from Ron
who knew karate and had touched a dead body.
Melbury Street: skinned knees and Dunlop Volleys,
cold war cartoons, meat and no veg
unless you count chip potatoes.
Melbury Street: houses all split
down the middles, two in one, all the same shape
and layout, same size, same colour, same bricks,
same wire fence and concrete drive.

Blew my mind, at five,
when Mum took me visiting her friend
in town. The house had stairs
and a brush fence.
You couldn't see the neighbours.
The rooms were different,
the yard was different,
the roof was different,
the windows were huge, and the TV too.

17

The boy who lived there knew piano
and said dead bodies were full of germs.

Driving away, other houses were different too,
most two-storey. I felt dwarfed, worried
those strangers were there, watching.

But when we pulled up home, back to normal,
I didn't feel it. Instead I noticed how flat the place was
with its low rooftops, how exposed.
In town people got whole houses; we had to share.

Melbury Street: telling your front door by the car on the lawn,
your car by its dents, stickers, scratches.
Melbury Street: falling asleep to raised voices,
bass drum thumps and smashed glass cymbals.
Melbury Street: life looping round like the backdrop in a
      cold war cartoon
– do they think you're too dumb to notice?
Melbury Street: you must be too dumb to notice,
you're part of it, no different from any of the other fleas
down here on this dog leg, down Melbury Street.
You belong here. You are Melbury Street
and Melbury Street is you.

At nineteen I moved out. Barely five streets, mind.
And though it was no longer Melbury Street, of course
it was still God damn Melbury Street.
Just like every place I've ever lived has been Melbury Street
and now, at 4am, I'm standing, shivering, on Melbury Street.
Like the old cartoons, I always come back
to Melbury Street. Everything always comes back to
      Melbury Street.

That old house, brown grass, dented Corolla,
I wonder if it's some kid's first car,
if it's been or will be the scene of all those other firsts.
I wonder if he worked all summer to buy it,
in some shitty restaurant, some shitty uniform,
keeping silent while his boss told him he was no good
no different, going nowhere.
And did he believe it? Does he stomp on every single crack
down Melbury Street? Will he leave at first chance?
And will he come back? Will he stand here, shivering,
suddenly sober as 4am becomes 5am?
Or will he make it, somehow – escape
from Melbury Street?

All For You, 2005

My friends used to ask what I saw in you
and honestly, sometimes I asked myself.
I could never quite answer 'til that day
– or was it night? Time's over now –
I came home and it was gone,
along with you, our children,
a few books and the rest of my life.

Your note said you felt trapped,
that the house I'd built you felt more a prison.
Meanwhile I'd become something frightening,
you didn't know me anymore.

But I only ever gave what you said you wanted.
You asked for walls, thick and tall, so I built them.
I lived inside them too.
You said you needed protection,
so I became something frightening,
growled and defended you as best I knew how.

If you ever said you didn't like it
then I guess it was too hard to hear
through those walls,
over all that growling.
Or maybe you couldn't even say it,
same as I couldn't say –

I would have built any house you asked for,
become any kind of man.
But in fact you needed neither. That was the knife.

You cut me adrift as you cut yourself free
because I'd come to rely on those walls,
come to rely on you relying on me.

Whatever it was I saw in you,
I guess you finally saw it in yourself.

Haunted, 2006

(for Jason Silver, 2001-2005)

Always the quietest guy on the floor. Still,
through the whole chorus line of production
I could tell, you weren't one of their machines.

Always good for a beer. That was the problem
with both of us. No it wasn't.
But it makes a nice story.

We could have been winners, could have been right.
We'd have climbed beyond banks, bills and bosses,
shown them all — if not for the booze.

Yeah right. If not for the booze
you and I would have worked shit jobs,
loved the wrong women, died
too young and grown too old, respectively.
If not for the booze we'd have had no window, ever
to open, albeit briefly, no breeze
beyond that factory floor.

We might never have betrayed ourselves
as poets, never landed atop that sick black bike
with no brakes — five years
of screeching, smoke-stack showing 'em.
And I'm still not sure I'm glad of it.

It wasn't the booze that stuck you inside
those white sheets, that warped sideshow,
squeezed your mind through ever tighter hoops.

Your father sowed the seed when he said no way.
Your mother watered it, fed on the fruits
for twenty years, stripped you bare.

You bounced back — that first time —
What doesn't kill us makes us stronger. No
it doesn't, not in towns where people talk.

I watched them stick their little plastic dicks
in your arse. I should have stopped it,
but they had stethoscopes and I was just me.

I let them shoot their sickly loads
of sanity, spray salt on all your shorn off skin,
let them pickle you, a fish, mouth open inside glass.

I let them blow you up, deflate you,
again and again, 'til you burst,
'til the guts of it splattered all over.

And them? They just changed their gloves,
shrugged, whistled and walked away,
calm white ghosts.

Some people are dead before they even get born.
Others get dead fast so they can work and fit in,
but you just didn't know how.
You never were,
never will be one of their machines.

Token Bukowki Poem, 2007

*(after re-watching the 1987 film **Barfly**)*

At eighteen I wanted to be you
because you looked like Mickey Rourke
and you walked like Mickey Rourke
– shoulders hunched, but not for lack of confidence –
you had a smart line for every situation,
delivered with a left hook of a smile,
just like Mickey Rourke's
and you got women, women, women,
you and Mickey Rourke.

Shame I didn't know 'til years later
that you hated that film, hated Mickey Rourke
for giving you that confidence, that baby face.
Shame I didn't know you never got laid 'til 23,
that the women, women, women
were only after you were published,
that you stayed outside the high school dance
with toilet paper round your head, the blood
from your scratched acne seeping through, blossoming
red and yellow, carnations in a field of snow.

If I had, I might've wasted the best years of my life
on things I at least knew were meaningless,
might have learned more about cars,
become union rep like Dad,
might have kept my job,
married a girl who read her stars in Cleo,
might have done any hundreds of things that weren't poetry.

But no. I wanted to be you.
You who drank yourself sick, chasing bitter women, writing
    bitter poems 'til the bitter end.
And the joke is, even you never got to be you,
even Mickey Rourke never managed to be you
or even his silver-screen version. Poor Mickey Rourke
was never even really Mickey Rourke
– that 1980s rough diamond Mickey get the women,
    women, women Rourke –
by mid-90s just plain rough no movies Mickey face like a
    boxing glove Rourke.

You might have liked him better
if they'd made that movie now.
Except now, if they'd made that movie, Mickey Rourke
    would've been Matt Bloody Dillon.
So the punch line comes south paw,
from where I never glanced.
This is all I ever wanted. To look like Mickey Rourke
and get as many women, women, women as you
– a teenaged, toilet-papered you –
swilling bitter whiskey and writing
bitter poems 'til the bitter end.

Reflection, 2007

I could break you,
but I'd never escape you:
the worn pathways of your face,
wrong turns
and bloodstained highways
all winding back
to the same dead end –
broken windows grey eyes
gone pink now,
you sissy,
you galah.

Your stained teeth tell of late nights
and those black-no-sugar mornings after.
Your nose, like your politics, has copped a beating,
points right as if to spite you.

No more of those women with their waists,
their wide eyes and easy laughter
– though there are women, still,
women with memories of waists,
eyes blurred, too tired for laughter.
You feel like slapping them

for not slapping you,
except you're busy
burying your head in whatever sand lies waiting.

It's not that you don't learn from your mistakes,
you just keep finding new ways to make them.

Shannon Woodford

1979 –

The only Red Lion not raised in Elizabeth, Woodford claimed that other open mikes were "too conservative". She formed a relationship with Lind and lived with him from 1999 – 2005, during which time they had two children. Woodford now resides in Gawler where she balances writing with motherhood and a job in a nursing home.

Threw the Looking Glass, 1997 (Villanelle)

Here in this city of stick-on stars,
this city of corners and concrete trees,
i went and threw the looking glass

at all of the faces in all of their masks
leaping shop to shop, ravenous fleas,
here in this city of stick on stars.

Seven years' bad luck. (Stick that in your farce.)
This maze is more than wine and cheese.
That's why i threw the looking glass...

...and Oh! How lovely, a big fat blast:
billboards quivering, down on their knees,
here in this city of stick on stars,

this city of slow deaths that pretend to be fast.
Nothing is everything is never always as it seems
and me i went and threw the looking glass

because if this is The Answer i want questions. i pass!
i'd rather my sadness, my nightmares, my dreams.
Here in this city of stick on stars
i went and threw the looking glass.

Photograph, 1997 (Sestina)

Darling daughter, you could be so beautiful
if you only tried. Come on, smile for the photograph,
make like God's in his heaven and everything
is blah blah blah. Why do you listen
to that horrible music? I'm sure it's the reason
you got so moody and cut your hair.

I really wish you hadn't cut your hair!
Those long braids, they were beautiful.
(But of course I can't make you see reason.)
Just look at yourself in this old photograph:
so cute! In those days you used to listen
to my advice. You did everything

I ever said. Absolutely everything!
And you had such shiny hair.
But no, don't start, I can't listen
to these things you say. It is not beautiful
to embrace such emotions. I just want a photograph
of my happy family. I don't need a reason.

Sometimes I think you've lost all reason!
You want to throw everything
away like the cut heads in that photograph
you ruined just like you ruined your hair.
No, I don't believe anybody could find it beautiful.
For once, for God's sake, just listen!

30

You and your father, you never listen.
Is it drugs, is that the reason
why you don't want to be beautiful?
Why do this, when we've given you everything
you could ask for. At least brush your hair
and stand straight for the photograph!

Because I just do, I want a happy photograph.
Why tell you why? You won't listen.
You never do. Why don't we dye your hair
blonde again? That ugly colour is the reason
you don't have boyfriends. But everything
will be right if you let me make you beautiful.

Because that's what life's about, being beautiful.
If you are then you can have everything.
Please. All I want is a photograph.

Eating, 1997

Eating is not an activity,
but a place i take myself:
a cave where nobody can find me
(even me (especially me)).

Eating is its own identity,
a complete identity, the only identity
that's ever fully fit
and even offers room to move.

i'm free inside here
and so warm.
i'm not just eating, no,
i am eating

and eating is me
and i am being
eating and eating is
eating is eating

up until everything is
eaten out, it's over
and i'm out, once again:
no my, so much self...

Black Jonquils, 1998 (Sonnet)

You sent me flowers and it freaked me out,
i asked myself, what is this guy taking?
'Cause i'm not the sort they write poems about,
so forgive me if my hands keep shaking
when you hold them, 'cause i'm just holding on
to this dream that somehow stays when i wake.
Still, i don't dream it can last very long
(Surely it's a joke, a set up, all fake...)

But even if that is the real story,
even if i wind up blue, choked on tears,
even that won't change the fact you held me
and for those moments, we laughed back at fear
'Cause you were freaked too, i tasted the sweat
on your palms, like a fortune or a bet.

Aspartame, 2003 (Villanelle)

i'm yet to master the art of tea with mother
in my lounge room, bald carpet and stained walls,
her body rigid, pearl earrings and lashes aflutter.

Five years old, i spray crumbs and stutter
as Rottie bounds up with a wet tennis ball.
i'm yet to master the art of tea with mother.

She declines my biscuits (too much butter)
sighs as she negotiates toys in the hall,
her body rigid, pearl earrings and lashes aflutter.

i've learned not to mention my significant other,
but when my three year old says "bloody," i recall
i'm yet to master the art of tea with mother.

She finishes her cup. No, won't stay for another.
i wonder inside why she comes here at all,
her body rigid, pearl earrings and lashes aflutter.

It's in my throat, but i just can't say, Fuck her
and her blonde bob, her BBC wannabe drawl.
i'm yet to master the art of tea with mother,
her body rigid, pearl earrings and lashes aflutter.

The Care Factory (Villanelle), 2004

After a few weeks, you forget the smell,
forget all your no-lift training
and the woman who screams she's in hell.

You learn not to hear the ever-ringing bell
The first rule of Aged Care: don't. (Too draining).
After a few weeks, you forget the smell.

The old man hit you, but it's your fault he fell.
The charge nurse gives you a shaming
and that woman still screams she's in hell.

One hour to toilet twenty people. How to tell
which ones really need changing?
By this stage you've no sense of smell.

Still, you smile, pretend everything's well,
pretend that your back isn't straining,
you can't hear that woman, screaming she's in hell.

Your arse pinched is part of the job, so don't yell,
don't show how your patience is waning.
After a few weeks, you forget the smell,
forget you're a woman, screaming, in hell.

The Australian Dream, 2005

i'm home, arms full of groceries.
You barely move, transfixed by TV.
The letterbox is bursting with bills,
the sink with dishes.
We nuke cold pizza, wash it down with beer.
There goes my diet.

But tomorrow, i'll start a new diet.
Why did i get Tim Tams with the groceries?
The thing is, i don't even like beer,
don't like whole nights in front of the TV.
Tomorrow i'll wash those dishes.
Tomorrow i'll pay those bills.

Except there's no money for bills,
nor for those shakes that help you diet.
Turns out i can't do the dishes
because i forgot detergent (time for more groceries).
Meanwhile, you're watching models on TV.
i think i need a beer.

Or maybe three beers.
i'll use the credit card to pay those bills
and to buy those shakes from TV.
Success guaranteed!* Plus a free book on diets.
Shona wants Coco Pops next time i do groceries.
i say, okay, if you wash the dishes.

And as usual, she breaks half the dishes
while you just break open more beers.
i take a breath, unpack the groceries
and open the credit card bill...
i feel dizzy, must be this dumb diet.
i need Tim Tams and TV.

Except there's nothing on TV.
In the sink, a new pile of dishes.
Tomorrow i'll start a new diet.
This is my last ever beer.
No more credit card bills,
no more unhealthy groceries.

But there's Tim Tams on special every time I do groceries,
in the letterbox, two more bills
and would you believe? We're out of beer...

Destroying The Matrix – A Nonnet, 2005

Your love was the red pill and i took it.
A crowded bar, a glance, a song, a smile...
grabbed your hand, oh yes, sweet damn, we shook it.
We were heroes, villains, free (for a while)
unplugged from the web i'd called my childhood,
the web i'd called my life, at last, i danced
and happily declared myself no good,
swilled rum with you and Morpheus, i chanced

to glance in the mirror one blue morning
and saw my mother staring back, a hack-
-er in the system i thought i'd shut down,
a bright red and purple flashing warning.
But still somehow i ignored all the cracks
in that Brave New World we'd built around us,
kept right on swallowing those pills, pawning
my dreams for a dream land, too scared to pack
my bags, to open my eyes for real and see red.

Gawler Central (Pantoum) 2005

i guess i've reached it:
the end of the line.
A muffled voice keeps saying,
"last stop, Gawler Central…"

The end of the line,
oh so old, oh so cold, all alone.
Last stop, Gawler Central
at 11pm, got to walk through dark.

Oh so old, oh so cold, all alone.
Still wanting you, your warmth
at 11pm, got to walk through dark,
the kids sleeping (wish i could).

Still wanting you, your warmth…
Why did i ever leave?
The kids sleeping. Wish i could.
i remember sleeping in your arms.

Why did i ever leave?
Why did i stay so bloody long?
i remember sleeping in your arms.
i remember how it hurt.

Why did i stay so bloody long?
i've forgotten the way it felt to love.
i remember how it hurt.
Never thought i'd end up here.

i've forgotten the way it felt to love
myself – did i ever know?
Never thought i'd end up here,
at the end of the line.

myself – did i ever know
that person? In the mirror,
at the end of the line.
Nah. Beyond it, but.

That person in the mirror
– me – i'm broke, but not broken.
Nah, beyond it. But
the end might be the beginning, y'know?

me, i'm broke, but not broken.
A muffled voice keeps saying,
the end might be the beginning, y'know?
i guess i've reached it.

Rude Awakening, 2006

(for Jason Silver, 2001-2005)

The first time I met you we drank red wine
and swirled its epiphanies for hours.
We wrote poems together and it didn't matter what they
were called, or how long the lines went.
It all seemed too good to be true.

You let me climb aboard your dreams,
shiny, black and lethal,
helped me brush the dust off my own.
You showed me endless highways beyond

my four-room world of bills and broken promises.
All the promises I'd broken to myself.
You made me believe I might still mend them.
With you there was always a way.

Always a way to mend everything, but yourself.
Months later, in the hospital courtyard,
smoking patched end-cigarettes,
you sounded so different.

Washed out, your white ghost gown
couldn't hide the protruding ribs, the scars
all over that dull-eyed sour-smelling you
I couldn't quite believe was you.

But come springtime you were back,
arms full of jonquils. We wrote poems
and dreamed journeys all over again
except by then I knew it really was too good

to last. But damn, we rode those dreams
all the harder for knowing.
You taught me the blank page is an open road,
leading to any place you dare name.

Taking each corner at top speed, it wasn't the end
that surprised me, but that it lasted as long as it did.
You always lived too fast for this slow-death world,
you were always too good to be true.

The Things You Didn't Have, 2006

You wanted me to have the things you didn't
when you were a child in the Northern suburbs,
growing up with no money, no Dad:
ballet lessons, blonde dolls and pretty dresses.

When you were a child in the Northern suburbs,
you never dreamed any daughter could hate
ballet lessons, blonde dolls and pretty dresses,
seeming so god-damned perfect.

You never dreamed any daughter could hate
a mother who stayed with her father
seeming so god-damned perfect
(the hair, the nails, the house, the car, the smile).

A mother who stayed with her father,
the thing you dreamed about most of all.
The hair, the nails, the house, the car, the smile
a full-time job that wore you down.

The thing you dreamed about most of all,
was the thing i ran away from,
a full-time job that wore you down.
i swore things would be different for me.

Was the thing i ran away from
the same then as it is now?
i swore things would be different for me
and my children, money or not.

The same then as it is now:
we're so similar in our differences
and my children, money or not
hate me a little, as is normal.

We're so similar in our differences:
my faded black eyes, your painted-over eyes
hate me a little, as is normal.
We've practiced silence as if it's a dance.

My faded black eyes, your painted-over eyes
don't blink, don't give anything away.
We've practiced silence as if it's a dance,
as if we couldn't read each other's minds. i've learned,

don't blink, don't give anything away.
You say you worry for your grandchildren
as if we couldn't read each other's minds. i've learned
love and cruelty are easy to confuse.

You say you worry for your grandchildren
growing up with no money, no Dad.
Love and cruelty are easy to confuse.
You wanted me to have the things you didn't.

Fat Is A Feminist Issue, 2007

(after the book by Suzie Orbach)

Fat is a Feminist issue
and by association, so am I.
Fat is a bodily tissue.
There's plenty of reasons why

we store it to keep ourselves safe
against famines and blizzards and pain.
In some cultures, fat equals beauty
and within ours I think it's a sane

kind of madness. Fat stands out
and fat hides. The word fat
packs a punch. Just three letters,
one syllable, yet it's huge.

It fizzes on the tongue, launches
like spittle, splattering your whole face,
stinging your eyes. To say, I am fat,
is to swallow it, to cough right up.

(i am fat and i am ashamed).
I am fat and I am proud.
(i am fat because i am weak).
I am fat because I am strong.
(i am fat because i deserve to be fat).
I am fat because I am fat.

My breasts are fat and my arse is fat.
I should be ashamed that they make me so proud.
I must be weak for letting myself get fat,
must be strong for pulling it off.

Some think fat is the end of the world,
not realizing that it too is round.
I am fat, and a hundred other things as well.
I am who I am (and I'm fat) and I'm glad.

Gifts, 2008

You gave me a flower
on New Year's eve:
blue-black, wet with moonlight.
It had no scent.

You gave me a whisper,
you gave me your skin
and I put it on like a fine coat.
It kept me warm.

You gave me waves and white foam
in the January heat,
gave me salt, the moon and seashells,
and all the things within.

You gave me shipwrecks and storybooks,
sharp rocks and the waves that melt them
down, down, we wrote it all down
so it could all wash

away. Red leaves, brown leaves,
grey smoke. You gave me
whiskey on the front porch,
a midnight that lasted two years.

Two years with twelve winters.
No snow. I wanted snowflakes
so you gave me broken glass
and I held tight, my hands weeping

red teardrops. You gave me a basin,
said to wash the stains away.
I stole an empty beer can
and hoarded them beneath the bed,

but come Spring there was no room left.
They sprung from the mattress
as jonquils, thorny jonquils.
Yelping and cursing, you gave me anger:

your anger, my anger; twins
conjoined, but not identical.
You smashed my head against the wall.
I whispered something that made you cry.

You gave me promises
and I buried them in the back yard.
Nothing grew.
You said you'd give me fire,

but I had plenty of my own.
I gave you back your skin,
stretched and fraying as it was.
I stood shivering like a hatched moth,

slowly figuring it can fly.
You gave me scars, you gave me whispers.
On New Year's Eve
you gave me a flower.

Angie Rawkins

1982 –

Rawkins was only sixteen when she attended the first Red Lion Reading. Having dropped out of school in 1998, she became pregnant in 2000 and gave birth to a daughter. In 2005, Rawkins began a Bachelor of Arts part time at Adelaide University. She is currently in her final year and plans to continue with postgraduate studies.

'I'm Not Gettin' On That Bike Wiv You', 1997

I'm not gettin' on that bike wiv you / That's right, you,
wiv yr greasy hair, yr green eye glare, & that tatt
ov a dragon I havn't seen / don' wanna / don' even know
it's there (where?) 'cause nuh-uh / no way /
you don' do it for me
in th slightest & Yes Sir I said No Sir-E-for-ever-and-ever-
amen / Need I say it again? I'm not not not
not gettin' on that bike wiv you.

& I'm not ridin' out to sea wiv you /
not gonna taste th salt air / nor th sweat
inside yr spare helmet / not gonna wonder
if it's yours, or... No / I'm not
gonna swim inside yr jacket / th leather so soft
yet so strong / not gonna hold on
to you for dear life screamin' little deaths
'cause there's a church tower between my legs
& it's ding dong dingin' kingdom come & I am
over/come/in' / synapses thrummin' / amped up
like a fat black bass guitar / baby / play it /// play it!
GRRRRRRRRRLLLLLLLLLLLLLLL! Th streets unfurl

as our bodies fall into one rhythm / one engine
as we sway together / stay together / thru all th soft sharp
grooves ov gravity & it's prob'ly not quantum physics / but
     Fuck
I don' care what is,
'cause right now th whole universe is all systems
GoGoGo!   /// I mean NO
/ no / no / I'm not gonna go /
I'm sure as hell
/ not /
gettin' on that bike wiv you...

They Say, 1998

*"You obviously put a lot of thought into this...
please leave your thinking for when you're not at school"*
– History Teacher

They say yr bad
for what you don' know /
badder
for what you do //

They say stuff's true
if it's printed in books
/ their books /
not th dusty things you pick up
in op shops like had-it hookers //
They say you got a lot to learn

but what they mean is
you got lots to forget //
Like th way you yearn
for knowin' / not knowledge /
dis / cover / y / s
not stale cracker facts //

They say yr not too clever /
they say don' be so smart /
they say you cld do so much better /
you've blown it /
you were hopeless from th start //

They say sit up! / they say shut down! /
march! / jump! / think! // shit! // don't think!
They say you oughta listen /
but they really mean make yrself deaf
to all th deaths you hafta die
to grow up / to live a big fat life //

Well I've got some things to say myself /
like that I'd rather speak
my mind than repeat someone else's /
& if I'm off th rails
least I'm not on yr hook //
I'll write my own formulas
for my own problems // I'll read
th world / that huge textbook
nobody can finish or even hold still //
Each face holds a lesson /
each moment a test
wiv multiple answers
// none right, none wrong //
I'll find th way that's best
for me // They'll see //
'Cause I don' swallow what they say.

Checkd / But Not For Free 1999

Th title Check-Out Chick
doesn' giv you permission to do so / bro /
so check yrself
& cut it out or y'll wind up checkin' in
to E.D. afta I get you chuckd
& pluckd like a chickn /
'cause I ain't smittn
by those chit-head lines
you prob'ly find in yr mornin' cereal /
no doubt eaten afternoons
wiv yr goons ov mates /
bongin' on & late for nothin'
'cause yr lives r just that / dross //
So what a cop out I can't get you kickd out //
Turns out yr in charge ov this check out //
A chump & a creep, but I gotta turn th other cheek
'cause replacements r cheap & rent's not / boss //

Blood Sucka, 1999

I was lookin' for somethin' /
didn't know what /
but I knew I'd find it that night //

I knockd off work /
knockd down three shots // felt right
not to knock back yr offer
ov a ride round th block
on th back ov yr bike //

Black-clad vampires / we gorged
on evry corner // Full throttle
in th full moon light //
& ice-ripe air made us hot/Hot/HOT/
for th scent that night //

What a shame everythin' afta /
quite frankly m'dear
turnd to shite //

Y'see I learnd a few things from my mother
& one was not to get playd
by fools // Did you think I'd drool
over I love you afta just one night?

So call me a slut if you must //
Afta all / I let you bite
my neck as I spread my legs /
& leglessly let go ov my body // but not my soul //
& hell sure not my mind //

As for my heart / that's just a muscle //
A strong one / you shld note

So don' say words you don' mean //
I don' care 'bout Fuck // Love's what's obscene //
I don' believe in it / but / some girls might //
Still / no hard feelin's /
we both got what we needed that night //

56

Dyin to be Alive, 2000

Every week I ask myself / Why
do I do it? / What's left
ov Sunday rear ends into Monday
TuesdayWednesdayThursday whizzin' past
fast as groceries 'cross th scanner
'til Friday rears up like a ferral skin condition
& I itch all over /
twitch & remember
that I do it for th growl
ov th zippers on my knee-hi boots
like Harleys at a red light
revvin' up //
I do it for th furl
my mirror givs me as I blot my bright pink
Why don' you buy me a Bundy?
I do it to remember who I am
when I've forgottn my name /
age / address / star sign...
but honey / for you I can be anything...
I do it for th slam
ov my heart against my chest
like cards on a table
'cause at 4am any fuck's a fairy tale //
Just takes one song
by Bon Jovi, & I'm half way there
// dunno where // but hell /
sure is some ride //

In Memory ov Me, 2000

I am not me /
anymore / never will be /
ever again // I am dead //
But instead ov a funeral

they giv me booties
& suddenly every loon
at every bus stop / book shop /
servo / Go-Lo & shop toilet
reckons it's their lot to cop a feel
ov this swell that's swallowd me /
this great flesh monstrosity
'bout which I shld be so fuckin' happy //

// No ciggies //
// No booze //
Can't even mourn right
// I'm in limbo //

floatin' 'bout wivout lungs /
lips / a voice to shout // No!
I am / not / fucking / happy //
It's plain to see
// just look at me ///
But nobody can / I'm invisible
except for th lump
& even that is not my lump //

There's a stranger in here
// Two strangers //

one a child /
th other a mother //
th unknown me I'll hafta be
when this chrysalis cracks /
when I giv birth

to myself //

Ever / Afta, 2001

"The passion for destruction is also a creative passion"
– Bakunin

Least I never lovd you /
least I got that bit right //
Least I never knew you / never had you
to lose you // It was just one night //

& a thousand bloody years /
planes fallin' from th sky /
end ov th world as I knew it / th start
ov two brand new lives //

But not for you // Yrs carries on
th same // No shameful stares /
no wonderin' how to wear
this body / stretchd & torn / worn
down by whispers // the Slut! the Whore! //
No movin' back wiv mum /
a child again / givin' in
for a shot at growin' up //

I no longer dream in my sleep /
instead dream ov it / all day // such long days //
then up six times a night //
But least I never lovd you /
least I got that bit right //

& I'll fight to be everythin' my girl needs
// No / I don't mean ours // I'll read her Poe /
not Snow White // We'll grow trees / fat apples // We'll bite
deep into th flesh of each day / not carin'
what God or anybody says //
When she wants to know 'bout you / I won't lie //
I'll tell her / Daddy was frightend /
like little boys r // So Daddy ran to hide /
not 'cause he was bad / just weak / a coward //
Mummy was frightened too /
but grrls r tougher // We gotta be //

Least I never lovd you /
how cld I in just one night? //
But myself / I do // My daughter / forever //
This part I know I'll get right //

Why There's No Point Buyin' Me A Drink Unless You Think I'm Thirsty. 2002

I am not a territory to be battld for & gaind /
nor some lurid story / washd down wiv pales //
I can't be mappd / can't be made
to stay th same any more than to change //
Call me strange / but I'm happy being

single /
a mother /
single /
getting older /
single /
with a vibrator /
single /
& / yes
// single //

/ on my own / never alone //

& oh / th shame / quite derrangd
that I don' care // I even dare
to laugh out loud / walk proud & shout
Show us yr tits!
at th beer guzzlin' blokes who think they got a hope //

But dears y'see

I've got someone special
// her name's me //

So if y'wanna conquer & claim
go play yr bloody Xbox games
& leave reality to those of us in check / mate //

W.M.D, 2003

We interrupt your regular broadcasting to bring you the
    following message...
!!!REMAIN CALM!!!
Stay inside your homes / offices / air-conditioned shopping
    centres // The government has received reports of a
    W.M.D. located in South Australia / But everything will
    be okay if you
// just // do // nothing ///
Do not go outside or into the pages of any books //
    Particularly poetry //
We repeat // Do not read poetry // Do not listen to poetry ///
If you are within the vicinity of poetry // at / say / a slam or
    pub reading // then we are sorry / it is already too late...

Hear that folks? // We're all gonna die! //
As if it's somethin' new //
Right here / right now / right in front of you / this is a
    W.M.D.
// a Woman ov My own Destiny //
Beneath these baggy clothes I've strappd on enuf thoughts
& words to blow this show sky high
& my shrapnel's gonna stick inside everyone
'cause I'm a Wanton Mad Delilah //
Won't March to nobody's Drum //
They can fire all th insults they like / Won't Make a Dent
'cause these Words are More than Decoration //
I Write to Make a Difference
& this World can't Mould me into Deference
'cause I'm a-Wake to their Means ov Distraction //
I Want More than plastic Deities /
Want More than stick-on Diamonds /

64

Want More than Department store stock take
because I've takn stock ov this Well-Masked Dictatorship
& I'm wonderin'
// Where's My Democracy? //
I Wield My Diction as a Weapon
ov mass Media Debunktion
& I'm a Woman who Minds bein' Dominatd /
a Woman who speaks her Mind // what a Danger! //
Must be a Wench wiv a Mental Disorder
// No //
but a well-Wicked Ms. Dissidnt / I'll pay
& what's more /
a Woman
ill-Mannerd enuf to Dream //

That'll Learn Ya, 2004

Th child who was once inside me wants to know
where dreams come from / & where do they go
when you no longer remember?
/ Where did they get th names for colours?
/ What if there were more
we cldn't see because we need words to believe?
/ Who decides which weeds r flowers?

// At one point I knew what makes th sky blue /
why th sea keeps eatin' th sand /

                                        spittin' it out
                          & eatin' it //
Somethin' to do wiv th moon

or its orbit…
              …. is Pluto still a planet? //

We evolvd from little microbes
that crashd down in a comet…

…or was that just TV? ///

I used to hav all th answers /
used to be so damn sure
where I was goin' //
Look where it got me //

Wherever those dreams came from / damnd
where they went // I've spent six years
sloggin' it / swipin' scanners / stackin' shelves //
Saved not a cent / but // But
still hell bent

I won't be brokn in
no matter how brought down //
Gonna keep my head high
so when this child from inside me asks
if school really matters / I can tell her
Why
/ & /
But Why.

About My But, 2005

Damn / I let one slip again
// no / not in that way //
wld hav been met far more kindly
than this remiss syllable / juttin'
from an otherwise cogent sentence
like visible panty line wiv a designer dress //

Th B / so obscenely curvd
as is th U / utterly vulnerable
to unkind utterances / overlookd / misunderstood
& then the T / final insult
stickin' in like too-tight undies /
a lime green G-string peekin'
from poorly-fittin' jeans //

It no longer matters
if th rest of th outfit was stylish //
May as well be th only word I said //
Hell / th word 'but' may as well be my head //

I wasn't bred into this world
of therefores and howevers //
When I hafta say "Foucault" / I think / "Fouc / ault!" //
But wasn't it him who said /

"those who are inserted in these relations of power, who
are implicated therein, may, through their actions, their
resistance, and their rebellion, escape them, transform
them—in short, no longer submit to them"

& that he was proud to be seen as a danger to the
intellectual health of students? [1] //

Magazines r always makin' women worry
'bout our backsides / bombardin' us
wiv curveless / bloodless crack childs //

Me / I'm secretly proud
ov my round / protrudin' booty //
I'm not gonna change th things I say…
I might find new ways to dress them, though.

[1] Truth, Power, Self: An Interview with Michel Foucault (25 October 1982)
http://www.scribd.com/doc/16667145/Foucault-Michel-Truth-Power-Self

Legend, 2006

(for Jason Silver, 2001-2005)

If poetry is th hand-scrawled graffiti
on th brick wall of all we're told to be /
then you were th guy who climbd higher
than any other / stared straight
in the face of that corporate hire
ark of beasts & spat
yr fat visions in their eyes / aerosol fire //

Those beasts can bellow / but they can't reach
th words you burnd into th flesh
of their skyline / can't scrub the blood
from their Alpha Bet / th blood
that's splatterd all over their faces / th blood
that stinks out their private places / th blood
that never frightend you one bit //

One day we'll drink beers
& laugh at their arses / long gone //
Because you / my friend / live on
not just as words on paper /
nor even out loud / but in th lives
& minds of those who read them /
who scream them from towers far
& wide / on th in & out sides,
those not afraid to gather up fragments
of your black feather wings /
to dip them in ink / find a high ledge
& write //

The Death Of Art, 2006

(for Harold Bloom)

This is The Death Of Art //
I'm holding th corpse in my arms /
we're dancing / spinning / kicking dust in th air
to remind ourselves / we were & will be stars //

This is The Death Of Art and it ain't pretty //
Hell no it's beautiful /
more beautiful than a shot of whiskey / straight
& that shudder that sears through after // Oh // Yeah // This

is The Death Of Art & it's a little death
which is to say it's bigger than th whole damn nation //
It's going off! // & we're on for th ride //

This is The Death Of Art & it's got an engine
like a big boom volcano //
This is The Death Of Art & it's coming down/Down/
    DOWN like a wave //
This is The Death Of Art / but first it's gonna get naked //
This is The Death Of Art & it'll pump you
like ten tonnes of lead ///

Elvis died on th toilet //
Marilyn died on th toilet //
Michelangelo died on th toilet // No // He didn't //
But does it make any difference? //
This is The Death Of behind-glass Art & th birth
of breakneck breaking out //
The Death Of Art is a moral concern

far graver than th deaths of child soldiers
// which includes all soldiers //
This is The Death Of Art / but it's not the fucking bomb //
This is The Death Of Art
& it tastes like th sweat on your nipples //
This is The Death Of Art / but hell / can you blame it? //

// Still outlived the bloody author //
//& truth miscarriaged at conception //

This is The Death Of Art & it's gonna sing
'til th fat lady can't //
This is The Death Of Art & it aint going on no machine //
It wants its ashes shoved in a can/n/on /
shot up as fireworks//
Yeah / the funeral will be a blast //

'Cause this is The Death Of Art
& it sure as hell don't wanna be mourned //
This is The Death Of Art / but it don't matter
because death makes life //
This is The Death Of Art & it's about to rain down / black
    & burning //
This is The Death Of Art / & me / I'm hoping for scars //

Femme Fatalities, 2007

First they tell you you're too young /
th sun don't shine out your dot /
you upstart snot // as if you didn't know
from th start you were a dumb hussy tart /
as if your own family hadn't told you
night after night 'til you got up /
went out & proved 'em right //
bleached blonde hair / skirt to there /
since you couldn't be a good girl / grrrl
you got real good at being bad /
kept kicking down doors 'til they saw

much / much / More

than a quick screw / you blew
more minds than cocks
& that's saying something //

So now / having stuck in this game
all these years / bucked lame accusations
// all th doubts / all th fears //
finally / they tell you
you're too old //
They ain't sold on your tits
& other used bits
& it shocks them / always / when you smile
& say Thank You

'cause you're still kickin' down those doors /
still getting' th applause /
might not be hot / but damn / you're on fire //

73

New girls come on the scene:
fresh-faced / eyes stuffed with dreams
& you wish you could help them

'cause you know th lot they've got to cop //
& this part's what's really dumb //
you gotta stop yourself from saying
You're too young...

My Promise, 2007

(1)

When I was five years old / my mother /
lips scarlet
with blood / front teeth on th floor / promised me,

she would never fall in love again //

Now I am twenty-five /
older than she was that day / still such a child //
My own daughter is six / thinks it's fun helping Nan do her hair
& decide what to wear //
They listen to th Stones / tell secrets & giggle
while I sit next door / trying to study //

"What time will you be home?" I ask //
Mum just laughs /
her cheeks flushed / dress short /
lips scarlet //

(2)

After a few weeks she brings him home /
brings him into our home /
our home where we've lived / all these years /
just th three of us /
our home where we seem sisters
as much as mothers as much as daughters //
We lend & borrow roles
as if they were scarves or necklaces / all of us children
in a game of dress ups // at times even Lil plays parent //

Over dinner I pick at my plate /
pick th eczema on my knees /
but find I can't pick fault
with this accountant who likes swimming & doesn't drink /
this grey-haired man who smiles / asks me questions
about my study / about my poetry
// for crying out loud // & actually seems to listen
to my answers / to care.

So where do I get off /
getting miffed about my Mum being happy?
Am I jealous like a daughter
or a mother
or a sister
or just being a child? //

(3)

Her promise was never to fall in love again //
Mine was never at all //
I kept it twenty years / unbroken / though I bent it
& myself out of shape // I fell

in lust in lurve in fatuous infatuations / fell hard
& fast into strange beds / stranger situations / fell
for all th standard lines / fell off
th back of a bike once / th wagon on a weekly basis / fell
'til I could barely feel / fell over & fell out
with friends / got felled
by my fell-andering / flung
like so much flotsam / fell
'til my life was a free-fall free for all / a flustered flurry
of flings & fitful fumblings / I played
th fool / got felt up / told to belt up / fell pregnant /
felt sick every morning / finally didn't feel
like falling

(4)

Now Lil wants a boyfriend
except they all stink & drive her crazy //
I agree //

Getting ready's th best part of any date /
so we stay in & make up
our faces / style our hair & decide what to wear //
We listen to Pink / tell secrets & giggle // She asks /
have I ever been in love?

I say no /

not in love / but I love two people / two women
who teach & inspire me // & I love what I do //
If you have this kind of love then you can be happy /
which I am

& that's a promise.

Jason Silver

1971 / 2000 – 2005

Silver was supposedly an old workmate of Pete Lind's who could never attend the Red Lion Readings in person due to his ongoing struggle with Bipolar Disorder. After a series of breakdowns, Silver committed suicide in December 2005. He was, of course, fictional, one of at least two Australian poets who never existed in the flesh and possibly the only poet ever to have written posthumously. Lind, Woodford and Rawkins composed the poems and still refuse to disclose their methods or reveal who wrote what. They published Silver's collected works in early 2006. The work was highly acclaimed before the deception became known, but later dismissed as meaningless.

subtopia, 2001

scratched vinyl
a black snake swallowing its own
mornings: the dull clatter of a truck gobbling
the innards of bins: garbage, green waste
recycling
a DJ's remix
all the same old songs just the order changes
like a game of cluedo: whodunnit? where and how?
drag races: revving engines
a baby's cry
my mortgage my mortgage my mortgage my
mortgage mortgage mortgage – my!my!my!
a baby's cry
an invisible black
eye hurricane
swallowing its own
snake: remix: mortgage: morning: clatter
dull
paranoia
petrol
a baby's cry
whodunnit? where and how?
the innards of bins: green
waste / garbage
recycling a DJ's drag race
remixed engines
secondhand sofa: black snake
scratched vinyl

a girl i knew, 2001

i knew a girl who swallowed her own face
(a face who swallowed a girl (a faceless
girl (swallowed by what she knew
(what i (what everybody knew
and nobody knew
that girl who swallowed the i
she couldn't face (the her
she couldn't knew (a swallowed girl
who faced her own her (a swallowed face
who owned her own own ((i knew
that girl (knew her face as well as her face
because i never forget a face
(except when i do(((
(but that girl (that girl
(((((((((((((((((((((((((((((((((i knew

why i've stopped reading the newspaper, 2001

another day another nervous break
down in the global financial
systems of ones & zeroes
(& you suspect you're a zero)
tolerance policy on
& on & on again
off again a gain i gain
that this elevator's going down
but not on the likes of us, baby
bunting bye bye time to go
a hunting through the classified
(s)information is power is planted
bombs in every flower pot
I'm not not not
gonna spend my whole life down
in this mine shaft my mind
blasted politicians & their words
worth fuck all lonely cloud struck
a match & burned up
into the sky like if helios had a harley

houdini, 2002

Roll Up! Roll Up! Cum Marvel
At the man With No Skin

the man Whose Thoughts Flash
Like Neon Signs In A Downtown District

```
          *A*
          *D*                         *T*
                                      *E*
              *V*E*R*                 *A*
                                      *S*

              *I*
              *N*


              L  ST

          In Pale Pink Flickers.
```

Roll Up!
And We'll Roll him Out,
Reel him In With Our Big Wooden Pin. he Is
the man With No Skin. Watch

       As We Reach In, Re
       Arrange his Org
       Ans It's Such
       A Fun Game
       And such pretty
       Red
       Goop inside
       Him
       !

So Roll Up! It's Not Everyday You Can See a man
With / Out Skin
In This World Of Tamed Lions And Empty Cages.

there's no light, lenny, and that's not how it gets in, 2002

today, even the raindrops are cracked.
the radio has floaties
in all its songs. i want to freeze
frame the world,
but instead the world has framed me, frozen.
and cohen, groaning low through static oceans
couldn't give a shit. but not all misery makes millions.
if i could just keep my eyes open
long enough to see through even one
of those raindrops, i might read the secret
way to stitch this body back
together. or maybe crawl inside
a chrysalis made of stained ceilings
and guitars on shuffle replay. i might finally fly
out of this terrorist threat called skin, replay myself
as a riff or a raindrop
falling upwards. for once
I'd be the one without cracks.

Conversation Through An Unbreakable Glass Wall, 2002

You need to Stay Here
because you need to get Better.
You need to get Better
because you are Sick.
Yes. You. Are. Sick.
Why else would you Need these tablets?
You. Need. These. Tablets.
Because you need to get Better.
Because you are Sick
Because. That's Why You're Here.

rosie n me, 2002

rosemary kennedy asks me for a cigarette
and i say, "get lost panda head,
your folks got the money to buy 'em".
she sighs and starts to shuffle on; i see
the tears she can't cry anymore
hanging lead chain heavy round her neck.
i say, "alright rosemary, but
you have to give us a kiss".

she pauses
blinks
a few times
then nods

and plucks out an eyelash.
"make a wish".

i close my palm, open it
to find a sharp blue shard of broken glass
"from the window to my soul", she mutters
and i bleed a little so she knows
i'm kissing her back.

we light up

our cigarettes
– church candles, memorials
for the dead, our selves.
together we pray
for cancer.

Element Number 3, 2003

Jesus didn't want Kurt for a sunbeam,
So what hope a wretch like me?
Amazing Grace, how sweet the taste,
That set me free from free.

Each week I make my confessions,
To the priest with letters on his name,
With his pen he impales my demons,
Readies me for the kingdom of the sane.

Tremors, flab and tiredness,
My body becomes my penance,
It is salt, not bread I swallow,
In the hope it will bring deliverance

From the fires inside, their searing light,
And the dark that light uncovers,
The dark that sang across oceans afar,
My sweet, sadistic lover.

I'm a fugitive now, new name and all,
The priest hung it round my neck,
I say it over and over, my rosary,
"I like it, I'm not gonna crack."

extractions, 2003

my priest is a kind of dentist.
he sits me in his chair,
tells me to open wide.
and if I won't
or can't
there's novocaine aplenty.

brandishing ice picks, he pokes
and prods inside me, scratches
and scrapes and exclaims
with delight
at yet more rottenness, ripe
for extraction.

he	is	pul
ling	me	a
part		piece
	by	
piece,		ham
mer	ing	my
head	in	to
a		bag
	of	
blood		and
	bone	

but he is a good, kind man, my priest.
and if i am a good boy,
if i lie real still and don't complain,
he will make me a smile
out of pink and white plastic,

a straight, shiny smile
like the one i never had.
if people don't look close
 – and people don't –
they'll think it's real.

now it strikes me
on the bus, at the shops,
every minute, all around –
hundreds of people all smiling
straight and shiny
pink white plastic smiles.
they make me want to shout hey!
to clink teeth together, a toast.
but no. i can't
let them know
that i know
that they know
even though i know they do.

each night i slide my smile
from my gums,
still bleeding,
soak it in salts for eight hours.
eight sweet hours.

Moniker, 2005

My Name is My Name
is not my name.
it is the name of other people
dead and alive
alive and dead.
My Name is a name
(is a word (is
several symbols (a widely
known code (an invention (a game)))))
My Name is a sound,
an evolved grunting. I
am My Name,
but My Name is not i (am
a cluster of cells, a series of electrical
impulses). My Name
is tied around my wrist
unlike my name (which i hold tight
inside myself, a smuggled drug,
too sweet to take).
My Name is a command
to which I answer (but i don't)
a set of walls in which to assemble
white goods, sound systems, garbage
disposal systems and all
the other systems, the flat pack essentials
of that modern Me
(which will never be me).
My Name is My Name
is very important,
but it doesn't matter what it is.

pOst humOurOus pOem, 2006

i am speakh
ing to You from beyond
the page (be)yond cons
piracies called flesh & pol
ichtal fact
ions, though not be
yond the cunst
ravelling called   )langu(
age   (there is no esc
                                    ape from that(

like Judas
back from The dead
for a final cur
tained
caul
it self indulgents
my poked-out 'I's see far
ther than an
y of those muthas &
the end is no / longer
        where / than it was
in the beginning

y'see that ol' noose has made me ha
rd now so much harder
than any prick
ly little pen – y'know?

(y'no.)

if floggin' a dead
man seemed tiring, man, go
od luck with one who was ne
ver al
I
ve

Recent IP Poetry

Maisie and The Black Cat Band, E A Gleeson
ISBN 9781921869440, AU$25

Letters to my Lover, Heather Taylor Johnson
ISBN 9781921869662, AU$25

Ultra Soundings, Duncan Richardson
ISBN 9781921869341, AU$25

Words Flower From One To Another, Amelia Fielden and Saeko Ogi
ISBN 9781921869587, AU$25

Water over Stone, Laura Jan Shore
ISBN 9781921869208, AU$25

Tongues of Ash, Keith Westwater
ISBN 9781921869266, AU$25

Men Briefly Explained, Tim Jones
ISBN 9781921869327, AU$25

Coda for Shirley, Geoff Page
ISBN 9781921869303, AU$25

Edge Music, Stuart Cooke
ISBN 9781921869426, AU$25

City of Possibilities, Jane Williams
ISBN 9781921869105, AU$25

For the latest from IP, please visit us online at
http://ipoz.biz/Store/Store.htm
or contact us by phone/fax at 61 7 3324 9319 or 61 7 3395 0269
or sales@ipoz.biz